BOOKS BY SAM HAMILL

poetry

HEROES OF THE TETON MYTHOS

PETROGLYPHS

THE CALLING ACROSS FOREVER

THE BOOK OF ELEGIAC GEOGRAPHY

TRIADA

ANIMAE

essays

AT HOME IN THE WORLD

anthologies

MID-WINTER BREAK-UP

YESTERDAY'S FACES (with K. West)

animae

Sam Hamill

animae

COPPER CANYON PRESS

Illustrations by Ed Cain

Copper Canyon Press
P.O. Box 271
Port Townsend, Washington 98368

To my mother
Freeda Empey Hamill

"I want no more than to speak simply, to be granted
that grace.
Because we've loaded even our songs with so much
music that they're slowly sinking
and we've decorated our art so much that its
features have been eaten away by gold
and it's time to say our few words because
tomorrow the soul sets sail."

—George Seferis

Preface

In 1977 I began the study of classical literary Mandarin using Creel's *Classical Literary Chinese by the Inductive Method*, a text which forces the student to begin by translating. The initial volume was a translation of the *Shiao Ching* or *Classic of Filial Piety*. Later that year, my adopted father died following a lingering illness. He had taught me my first poems, poems I memorized immediately after I was adopted at age four. I have retained the utilitarian view of poetry I inherited from him.

Simultaneously, I began to re-evaluate certain political assumptions, namely the issue of 'feminism' as I understood it. I had always thought myself a 'feminist,' but had grown suspicious of my own poems, poems that exhibit a traditional 'hardness' that is associated with the masculine stance of so much American poetry by men. Following several conversations with Olga Broumas, I began rereading the important work of Adrienne Rich, Susan Brownmiller, and others in hopes of finding that which is feminine in myself.

Jung points out that deep introspection and ecstatic experience reveal the existence of a feminine figure in the unconscious. In naming this figure, he resurrects the archaic Greek term, *anima*. And Richard Wilhelm, in his translation of the *Hui Ming Ching* (*Book of Consciousness and Life*), says, "The sages set forth their thoughts about the unification of human nature and life by means of images from the external world; they were reluctant to speak of it openly without allegories."

These poems sprang from moments of meditation, deep introspection, and ecstatic experience. Although the autobiographical thread is obvious, I would hope these poems would not be considered "confessional" in the conventional sense; their urgency was, for me, that of direct utterance of sudden revelation, a convergence of learned and psychic experience.

Some of these poems, often in slightly different versions, appeared in the following magazines: Confluence, Silver Vain, Cutbank, Three Rivers Poetry Journal, Willow Springs, The Ark, Jeopardy, Urthkin, Spoor, The Anthology of Magazine Verse (1979).

"Dead Letter (I)" appeared originally as a pamphlet from Jawbone Press. "Reading Seferis" originally appeared as a pamphlet from Copper Canyon Press.

Several of these poems appeared in a chapbook, *Penumbra*, published with painstaking care by Barbara Barry at Uintah Press.

The epigraph from George Seferis's "An Old Man on the River Bank" is from the *Collected Poems* translated by Edmund Keeley and Philip Sherrard (Princeton University Press) and is printed by permission of the translators.

S.H.

CONTENTS

To Live and Die in Portland

I could tell you how
my whole life began
at sixty miles an hour
on the highway rolling
into Portland; I could say
I tasted the black kisses
of diesel stacks
all the way from Seattle;
I could describe
the paunchy woman
sobbing in her wine
alone at the bar
in a Portland neighborhood
tavern where everyone
memorized her sorrows
long before the rain began
in the dark streets
of November. And she,
she could tell you
how her husband
who has gone away
once farted in his sleep
or gulped a belch
at the breakfast table.

And I could say
how, drunk, I shivered
all night on a cold
linoleum floor
hugging a borrowed blanket,

and I could tell you
it ended in Portland
in a dawn without sun
on a day without warmth
whining a highway
home. But it began
a long while back,
in the memory of mesquite
and sand: it began
with circling winds.
It began with the telling
of stories, and good ones
lope in circles
and like circles
have no end.

I

"Worship the virtue of ancestors,
not ancestors themselves."

Kung-fu tse

Penumbra

It is not yet spring
in the country where the wind
hangs the many garments of its voices
from the dead limbs of trees,
where it uproots whole alders
and rattles young cedars
hard against the house.
The woman who has warmed my days
through seven years of poverty
and plenty slips down the ladder
to shutter a banging window
as I turn in my sleep, sweating,
toward the snowy blown arroyos,
the difficult beauty of my boyhood.
Wrapped in the wafting blanket
of my father's pipe tobacco,
I can almost breathe
the immense quietude of snow
blown among the cottonwoods,
I can almost smell the saddle soap,
the barley, oats, the cinders
we hauled out Thursday nights,
or my mother's rich brown bread
darkening in the oven.
                              A step groans loud
as Tree climbs back toward bed,
swaying through the penumbra,
the moon between the windows.
Beside the bed, our sheepdog
sighs and stirs. From her corner,

my daughter snores. A breath
heavy with sleep flutters across my cheek,
and I suddenly remember
that I am falling, that we
are all falling together, and that
the voices we remember, yesterday forever,
are all outside in their tatters
riding the surf of the wind, and that
if we listen closely
from the penumbra of our sleep
we all can answer their calling.

Otto Empey

My mother's father
was a working man. Coal miner or cattleman,
he lived his life by means
of his back and hands. The dangerous
black cigars he choked us with
were philosophy to him: he didn't give a damn
for kids or women, for city life,
and didn't care much for men.
I don't recall him ever
having a friend. Estranged
from his wife and daughters forty years,
his checks were regular, his visits
all on time.
                        Ott's only brother,
I heard tell, died in Moab, Utah,
backshot outside a saloon,
result of feud or brawl. But Ott
never mentioned him. Ott wasn't much
for talk. At night
when the valley faded into hills, he walked
the rows of chicken coops alone
or lounged around the porch.
                                        The tales
he never told, I made up on my own.
His lap I never sat on, I never dreamed
as I curled in my room. My mother
even now
remembers Ott in measured tones
and does not understand

how an orphaned boy and a stubborn,
unrepentant, ornery old man
dead all these years
could grow to be such friends.

Mae Empey

She married the cussedest man
in town. *Papoose*, they called her
as a child, and later simply
Poose until no one remembered her name.
Headstrong as any woman
of her time, her business sense
was sound. O handsome, strong
as her desperate land, she traded vows
with the only man
she knew she could not mend,
then fought with him
as only lovers can, divided, estranged
and still could not renounce
the vows they had exchanged. She sent
her daughters off to school.

When I was four, I staked
my own little corner
of her soul. Her hands by then
were paper thin, blotched by years
of sun and rain and snow. She lay
in her sickbed sheets
and raised her hand to brush
away my face, her fingers danced
like cobwebs in the dark
and sent a shudder I never could
disguise. When her eldest daughter married,
she dried her husband out
and carefully plotted the ground

where he would build a home. "A strange
woman," my mother says,
"but her business sense was sound."

In Sepia

A thin girl with handsome
boyish face, my mother
walks among cacti
in red sand and clay,
her gray eyes shy
as rabbits, her smile
old as stars that
will not go away.
It is 1922
and she's going away
to school. Her mother's
in the shadows, silent
at the station,
her strong desert bones
slowly baked to iron
by the Escalante sun.
My mother steps along
the ties. Her father,
squat and firm, a
rain-barrel of a man,
wears a black felt derby
squarely on his head,
his thick hands sweating
the palms. The mines
he lives to die in
beckon from the four
dark corners of his mind.
He sees a long way off
while waiting in the sun
for a train. Nothing's

there. My mother fidgets,
she notices how dust
settles down around
the plain brown shoes
scuffed upon her feet.

Prolegomenon

Up all night
with a hundred dying chicks
in the jaundiced light
of the coop, my father steps
into the first pools of day
pausing at the door
to scrape the dung from his boots,
leaning his back to the jamb
as he thumbs small curls of tobacco
into the burnt-out bowl of his pipe.

All night his ears rang
between the echoes of his heart
with the sickly *cheep, cheep*
of small white heads agape
from twisted necks,
beaks drooped open to ask
what no one ever knows, refusing
feed and drink as they died,
twisted in the palm of his hand.

And as the sun tears itself
on the blades of new roofs where
orchards he farmed once stood,
he strikes a match and draws deep,
and the gray mare ambles into dew
from the musky shadows of the barn,
her dark tail switching
the first flies of the day.

Squinting into the light, a pain
too subtle to name settles
in his chest, and as he begins
his chores, the morning
spreads over him like a stain.

The Egg

A round yellow light
peeps like a chick
from the round hole
at the end of a round
tin candler at the foot
of the steps in the musk
of a tarpaper cellar.
Six more beams silently break
from tiny holes at the back
which ventilate a bulb
inside. Hunched in that hint
of working light,
my mother candles eggs
picking each, one by one
from a basket, holding
each against the light
to look inside for blood
or other signs of life.
A hundred, a thousand eggs
each night, she takes
into her hands, cleans,
examines in the light,
and files in paper cartons
or in cardboard crates.

My father, stubborn, kind,
is out in the dark
of the coops, working
like a mule. My mother thinks
of him from egg to egg,

or of her borrowed son.
The work is slow, the light,
'though pale, familiar. Out
in the moonless night,
the cherry tree is bursting
into bloom, the first
green and waxy shoots
of spring break through
her tender crust
of topsoil. Her work,
she thinks, is good:
simple and essential.
She cleans and candles eggs,
the pure white eggs
of leghorns, every night,
packing away for sale
the spotless and the sterile,
keeping for her own
the tarnished, the cracked,
and the fertile.

Dead Letter (I)

Past midnight, rain
driven hard through trees
outside my cabin, I rise
from bed having slept
the sleep without rest,
the strange word still clumsy
on my tongue—*Father*,
I cried from nightmare,
Father, knowing no one
was there, knowing
no one ever would be there,
my own hair graying, and I
alone in another country.

Outside in the wind
black fists of rain
pummel the night until
the stars go out
one after another,
and I light the kerosene lamp
and huddle against the dark.
Father, I say out loud,
awake. And the wood
my own hands fit and nailed
whispers it back again.

Twenty years since I left
your house, and thirty
since your large hands held me up
and slipped me into the saddle.

Your hands were dry and red
as Escalante clay,
and the sweat of a hundred years
ran crazy down
the chiseled ravines
of your face. You told me then
you had more gold in your teeth
than in your bank account,
and you laughed
your great bearish laugh
to prove that simple truth.

How many years
since I stooped
in the icy mud of winter
above your unmarked grave,
not knowing how to weep,
unable to move, to speak,
to sigh. A mile north
where you farmed your life away,
the claws of the angry city
curled into soil,
and the soot of all the living
fell from a poison sky.

Tonight, in the light
of kerosene, it all comes back—
after dinner, after evening chores
when the stoker brims with coal
and with the blood of stewing hens
rinsed from your callused hands,
you lean back slow,

eyes closed, and sing
the song of Longfellow's Smithy or
the ballad of Sam McGee,
your voice as long and dark
as Timpanogos Cave.

But the stove that warms
these walls burns wood,
and the blood on my hands
is my own, and cannot
be washed away. I want you
to dry the sweat
of long bad dreams, to show me
how to say the things
I could not say
when I watched your beard
grow white and long
from a thousand miles away.

I blow out the lamp
and listen hard:
only the black rain falling forever,
only winds aching in the trees,
only the shadows annointing me
with shadows from the past.
Nothing lasts. And only hope
is free. Far off,
from the haunted cathedrals
of the narrow human chest, I hear
that old familiar drum
beat out its elegy.

Natural History

Late afternoon, autumn equinox,
and my daughter and I
are at the table silently
eating fried eggs and muffins,
sharp cheese, and yesterday's
rice warmed over. We put
our paper plates in the woodstove
and go outside:
                              sunlight
fills the alders with
the geometries of long
blonde hair, and twin ravens
ride the rollercoasters
of warm September air
out, toward Protection Island.

Together, we enter the roughed-in
room beside our cabin
and begin our toil together:
she, cutting and stapling
insulation; I, cutting
and nailing the tight rows
of cedar. We work in a silence
broken only by occasional banter.
I wipe the cobwebs
from nooks and sills, working
on my knees as though this prayer
of labor could save me, as though
the itch of fiberglass
and sawdust were an answer

to some old incessant question
I never dare remember.

And when the evening comes on
at last, cooling our arms
and faces, we stop
and stand back to assess
our work together.
                    And I
remember the face
of my father climbing down
from a long wooden ladder
thirty years before. He
was a tall strong sapling
smelling of tar and leather,
his pate bald and burned
to umber by a sun
that blistered the Utah desert.
He strode the rows of coops
with a red cocker spaniel
and tousled boy-child
at his heel.
              I turn to look
at my daughter: her mop
of blonde curls catches
the last trembling light
of the day, her lean body
sways with weariness. I try,
but cannot remember
the wisdom of fourteen years,
the pleasures of that
discovery. Eron smiles.

At the stove, we wash up
as the sun dies in a candle-flame.
A light breeze tears
the first leaves of autumn
from boughs that slowly darken.
A squirrel, enraged,
castigates the dog
for some inscrutable intrusion,
and Eron climbs the ladder
to her loft.
                    Suddenly
I am utterly alone,
I am a child
gazing up at a father, a father
looking down at his daughter.
A strange shudder
comes over me like a chill.
Is this what there is
to remember—the long days
roofing coops, the building
of rooms on a cabin, the in-
significant meal? The shadows
of moments mean everything
and nothing, the dying
landscapes of remembered
human faces freeze
into a moment.
                    My room
was in the basement, was
knotty pine, back there,
in diamondback country.
The night swings over

the cold Pacific. I pour
a cup of coffee, heavy
in my bones. Soon, this fine
young woman will stare into
the face of her own son
or daughter, the years
gone suddenly behind her.
Will she remember only
the ache, the immense satisfaction
of that longing?
                    May she
be happy, filled
with the essential,
working in the twilight,
on her knees, with her children,
at autumn equinox,
gathering the stories
of silence together,
preparing to meet the winter.

A Cold Fire

An hour after sunset
Venus hangs in the wintry mist
of the west, a cold fire
burning alone above wet trees
and hills that fall and rise
through the fog.
          We stand
together a long time
hand in hand
          watching
what we each have watched
a thousand times before.

Darkness and silence
join hands and spread
over us
        the cool caress
of their breath. There is
nothing to say, nothing
to do.
     Startled
into being something
we only dreamed of being,
we enter the exquisite
abyss of the first hour
before heaven.

Canto Amor

How many nights have we lain,
Love, side by side in a pool
of stars beneath the skylight,
dizzy from riding the turns
of the burning, vertiginous night.
Damp as the rain-soaked autumn
patina of moss outside, was it
the hush of desire fell over you?
No matter. The soft night sighs
of invisible animals hover
over our eyes, and our fingers
tremble, our breaths go out
into the dark on broken wings
that stagger through the trees.

Only the brightest of lights
burn inside: suddenly we see
each other illumined through
closed eyes and, dripping
the sonorous tears of long ago
remembered soft guitars, we
want to weep for joy, for
shame and sorrow together—
the pleasure, the weeping, the prayer.
The longing inhabits our flesh
like song, burns off into ash
the residue of pity. Come
with me now, Love, and enter
the ancient, human fire.

Burning, ache. Ache because there are
no love songs any more, because
there is no democracy of the soul,
because we must enter the grave
of the Twentieth Century heart.
We, we are the only flowers
we can bring. When we lie down
together in the dark, the Dead
sing, *Love, love*, and soft curtains
that frame the windows of our lives
become transparent, flutter,
and the old unnamable anima
shudders into life. As we look
out into the dark, its eyes peer in.

How many nights can we discover
ourselves in one another?
The immense sadness of the world
overwhelms. And yet we are here
beside the fire, beside the simmer
of the stove, needing no other.
Friend, or lover, comrade, partner—
we have commerce together. Tomorrow,
the world dies its daily thousand
thousand deaths. Tonight we die
into each other, into the mysteries
of falling light from stars
that died a thousand years ago,
that shower us with quick soft light,

that burn us beautifully tonight.

Dead Letter (II)

To love the dead is easy.
　　—William Mathews

Father, it is May again,
and I enter the thirty-seventh year
of my search. I have walked again
the long path through the woods
when ferns and ocean spray,
blackberry shoots and
the blossoming apple
wear the jewels of fine mist
into the afternoon. The juncos
this morning burst into song
shortly after four. I lay in bed
and listened. I remembered
the heavy silence of the Salt Flats
as we crossed them in the heat
of 1948, the sulphurous white teeth
of Kali grinning all the way
to Reno. If there are gods
of the desert lands, they are women
and angry and just. I have seen
in the heart of the Escalante
just enough life for hope:
hope for respite, for a better
life to come, or hope
to end a life of pain.

I watch the starlings chase
the ravens down endless ravines

of sky. Far below them,
the logged-off stubble and slash
of minds gone wild and narrow,
and I remember my grandfather,
Otto Empey, and I think
of what he never said, and of
the Taylors down in Moab, Lester's
great hands on the pommel
of his saddle astride
his buckskin mare. It is good work
that leaves us in the weather,
in the rains that fall
on all of us, living and dead
alike, in the blank snows
of memory that cool our dreams
and fill our lives with stillness.

And I can hear, coming
over hills of woods, the soft breath
of the sea. Here, in the country
of Chemekum and Makah
where rich robes warmed them
in winter, robes of cedar bark
and otter, where they brought down
their animals with stones
for maybe fifteen thousand years—
I am home. In the gray light
of early afternoon,
I can smell thistle and salmon
and the smoke of an alder fire
drifting over the dreamscape
of women and men and babies—

all who went before. I can hear
their chanting from far off,
from across the edge of the sea,
and see, perhaps, their longboats
slide across a bay. It is easy
to love the dead for what
they did, for what they didn't say.

When I gaze out far enough,
I can see where the sea meets
the sky—the dark approaches
that promise to return.
And as I turn toward my life
once more, it is the daily
I adore: the little pleasure,
the food and drink of necessity.
Down on Water Street, among
the fruit flies and oranges
and lemons, apples, and tangerines,
I'll pick among the artichokes
for one ripe and green, just right,
and boil it in water, and eat
the fleshy pulp of its leaves
scraped from around the thorns,
eat down into the soft green heart,
and remember you then who taught
me how, and then slightly bow
with neither praise nor blame,
and from my knees in the dusk
I'll pray once more for nothing,
for the dead,
and for the gifts they bring.

For the Anniversary of My Birth

Up before five, wakened again
by the trills of juncos
swarming through the alders,
and the gray dawn
comes on in a smear
that won't wipe away
the kisses of the dead
nor bad dreams turned real
nor the indelible handprint
of the damned that's plastered
in the air.
              I pee off
the high porch, stretch,
and spit last night's beer,
and scrub my mouth
till it hurts, till it
claws a burr from my tongue,
my tongue that tastes
of rotting leaves and ash
and the gritty damp
black soil that holds
us all in the end in
a last long clammy embrace,
that reminds us all that
we are small and foolish
and afraid.
              Yes, this is
America after all, and spring,
and I am alone where the sea
doesn't crash, doesn't fall,

but waits, patiently waits
for what the winds erase
on this anniversary of my birth:
another day, another hour,
another year.
                                  The factories
unlock their gates,
the cities blaze. If I walked
into the sea, it would
give me the salt
of its breath, the sighs
of the daughters of America
that I loved with an itch,
the cries of the sons broken down
in tears till I wiped
the snot from their noses
and wiped away their eyes, it
would give me the names
of all the grains of sand
that don't measure time
or measure out our lives.
It would give me time
to memorize my failures.
                                  But I
am here, shaken awake
on dry ground that won't
forgive my trespass nor
my slaughters nor the breath
I take each day
from its sisters the witness
trees. If I knelt in penance,
would the juncos laugh

until they cried, would
the trees quake, the clouds
roll on toward heaven? I'm old
enough to creak, but up
to meet the day for what
it's worth, for what I am—
small, impatient, per-
petually bending my back
in vivas for the damned.

II

"If there be a knife of resentment in the heart,
the mind will not attain precision."

Kung-fu tse

The View from Helicon

Sometimes, when the sea
grows unutterably blue,
and the sun resonates
with the residue of song,
and the day is green and clear;

sometimes, as the sea combs out
the dark fathoms of her hair
and the seasons stop to listen
as at equinox, vernal
or autumnal;
                  sometimes, when
the sea nymphs and the sons
of Helios gather on the water
to dance to invisible guitars
and flash their silver bracelets,

the world grows impossibly still,
small and quiet and attentive:
perfectly happy, almost
imperceptibly alive.

Mist & Clouds Over Mountains

Because it is morning, the sea
rises, the blue Olympics swirl
the clouds into paintings
by Wang Wei which reflect
the far side of the sea,
noumenal clouds forming steep
ravines of mist and mystery.
I remember I had dreamed
I was a woman in long semi-
transparent garments, gauze
perhaps, or fine silk, and
lingered in the candlelight
between two lovers. There was
nothing to it, just
the endless passage of time
no time can measure, the moment
stopped forever in my mind.
What pleasure. And awakened
in a soft landscape beyond
dreams and dreams of dreams.
Did I dream I was dreaming?
Was I my own lovers, languid
and satiate, are the mountains
more real because a human
voice has entered them?
Did Chuang tzu really fly?

To Kenneth Rexroth

Solstice. Once again
the foreshortened days
and cold clear nights
of winter.
       Last night
in freezing moonlight
I paused at the woodpile
where it lay under frost,
I paused to look up
at the Dipper.
       It hung
so close I could almost
taste its froth, and
suddenly, for no reason
I can name, suddenly
I remembered what you said
to Williams
       years and years ago
about a poet being one
who creates sacramental
relationships that last
always.
       The bare alders
glistened in the dark
and the whole world creaked
beneath my step. My own breath
wafted before me, and I
thought of how certainly
the diurnal becomes
the annual,

                    of how
the wood shatters
into flame as I stoke
the December fire.

Far to the south,
the moon pruned the tips
of Olympic cedars, then
slipped into snowy hills.
In this land you roamed
so many years ago,
                    on this coast
where you loved your grief
away huddled near a fire
on the cold beach at Kalaloch
under the floating shadows
of wooden sculptures carved
by the broad hands
of the sea,
                    we are at peace
in the world where
the dirty hands of Industry
find us too poor
to exploit.
                    Again and again
in this season's bitter
cold, I savor the sacrament
of your poems—always
the warm shadows of campfires
linger on,
                    odors of sheepherder
coffee, or moonlight

sifting the trees. The music
of silence drifts up
from the vast, soundless
sea.
   And in the flux and flow
of soundless change
unchanging, Adi-buddha
dances,
      and I am happily lost
in the dance of the Gopis
where only poetry is real.

Reading Seferis

To Olga Broumas

"Not many moonlit nights
have given me pleasure."
The stars spell out
the ancient mathematics
of the heart in huge
desolate zeros, ciphers
of nothing, and despite it all,
I care. There is a fatigue
in the crumbling of cities
for which there is no cure,
no penance or catharsis,
not even a prayer—only
the will to endure. The heavy
torpor of gray-brown air,
the lethargy of the soul—
by these we measure out
each crisis, each ancient debt
we don't repay the poor.

There are not many moons
I remember. The Sound
is blue where it reflects
the dark sky of night
or the bright sky of day.
Amica silentia lunae,
and each day the sun
drowns in fire and water—
a metaphor for nothing,

the unaccountable longing.
Some would call upon the moon
for power, for pure sexual
pleasure, but that is unholy
and denies both the sowing
and the reaping. The moon
is not a scythe that mows
the tall mute grass of heaven.

But we, Olga, are grasses
wavering in breezes
of politics and dollars, we
are the exiles of the earth,
the rooted and swarthy
who see the moon in everything
and think it a symbol
for our suffering. It is
the human mind that curves
into a razor, that harvests
human pain. We shall be
the chaff which flies
in the cutting, the lullaby
of the fields that is not heard
on moonless nights because
only moonlight is romantic.

I hear the lullaby of victims
who are happy. Few are the moons
for them, and even these
are imagined. I imagine the full
moon of a smile, the moon
of my buttocks when I was a boy

and a prankster, the twin
moons of my lover's breasts,
the stars, oh, in her eyes
and I love her. Olga,
these are the maps, topographies
of the heart that tell us
everything: we are all
the victims, we are heroes also
and slaves. Seferis says
the heroes are the ones
move forward in the dark.

I remember the terrible
darkness of my childhood
and the fear. And the moon
was more fearsome, more awe-full
with its wails and howls
and its shadows. I remember
the moon as female, Loba, yesterday
when she raged. I tire so soon
of metaphor! I want to send you,
Olga, the alphabet of stars
which ask for nothing
and offer a little light
against the dark we wear;
I want to offer the warmth
of a lullaby, the kiss of deep
sleep, a reflection of the moon
reflected on the waters
of your song—so few

are the moonlit nights
that I've cared for.

　　full moon
　　VIII:40079

To Kevin, Who Mourns

in memoriam, Jay Sisson
We see the weather unloading all its wares:
gray clouds, cold rain, and winds no one dares
to brave. The deep woods where Jaybird fell
are silent or they groan into shadows that swell
into a dark too deep to penetrate, too dense
to let a life escape. He died. What sense
we make of it or do not make, we feel
somehow betrayed, hurt or shamed. We kneel
beside a grave and weep for our own ensuing years
of solitude before the vague death we fear
grows friendly and familiar and the pain
of remembered deaths grows dim, a slight stain
spotting someone else's linen, we recall,
in the April of our years before the fall
winds blew the old gaunt Salesman in
to spread before us the wooden cross and tin
Jesus in his pain. We cannot buy the dead
another life. And yet we make them live, fed
by love, work and memory we freely give,
nourished by the weather of the lives we live.

Poeta del Pueblo

Kalispell, Hungry Horse, Coram,
Apgar, Glacier, and Nyack,
the long winter road
winding up from Missoula
to Browning under snow,

up and over the Great Divide,
and you're behind the wheel
squinting out at the frozen world.
When the boxcars rusty with abuse
rattle down from the tamarack hills,
you watch an artery of smoke
climb through crystalline air.

You are alone in your life
again, and driving hard
toward thirty. Next week,
it's classrooms in Missoula,
the junior high full of brats
that don't give a damn
about poetry. And when each night

you return, empty near broken,
to the cold cabin beside
the frozen creek, you have
time enough to think,
to remember it all as you shiver
beside a stumbling fire—

Brother, son of the sons
and daughters of Almeria,
son of the *goidel* bards
whose blood was spilt in Eire—

it is January, a new year,
and you have only the silence
of highways in the country
of broken treaties
with no one
to call your own. And because
you are alone with all the past
and all the future,

with nothing to call your own;
because you lend no part
to the cruelty of this world;
because we have seen you flame
into a word—because you do
without, my friend, poeta
del pueblo, everything you touch,

everything you kiss
with the echo of your breath
you make utterly new
and utterly your own.

The End of the Road from Nantucket

"This is the end of the whaleroad . . ."
   —Robert Lowell

I.
Dark. Dark, and winds
lash the rain into frenzy.
The whole continent sleeps
its bloody sleep of history
with dreams of Sitting Bull
and Joaquin Murietta,
keelboats and outcasts
from this coast of no story
all the way back to the glory
of Nantucket. The Orcas
cry into the Sound, rise
through dark-swirled water,
and plunge again, and still
the unappeasable fears,
the hard rain and wind
of desperate sea-locked men
ride out the winter storm.

II.
Dogfish slowly, slowly spin
beneath the waves. Friends, the
ancient gillnetter weeps
into the nets he mends. No mystery
to his craft: a lull
can promise fortune or get a
fisherman killed. What outlasts

the sea is praise. Glory
slides into a sailor's eyes all hoary,
weather-worn and wry, a cause-
way of human years. No Blighs,
no Ahabs survive to trouble water
on this coast. We will
ourselves no future, we steer
a course unmarked by dorsal fin
or blow-hole that gives again
and again each day a style, a form.

III.
Dark. Dark, and dark winds
swirl from the past. Wednesday
when we die, the sea will weep
no more, the lethal blistering
tides will rise into a full-
bodied swell lifting the last regatta
into doomsday, the masts
shattered like the Pequod's, forty
fathoms into hell. For we
who have no past or cause,
the seas fill our eyes
with the hunger for slaughter,
a taste for the manly thrill
of whaleblood, the sea's veneer,
of dying whales that win
no wars, no time, no gain.
It's a human name we give the storm.

While Galway Reads

In the atrium, where his
voice plunges into the dark fathoms of nightfall
and beyond, three new fathers pace
their babies, rocking as they walk
back and forth, heads cocked to listen
to poems that echo about them, that break
over them in waves opening
like the tiny pink hands
of their babies that sleep in their leaden arms.

And then a mother climbs
slowly up the aisle
to relieve her husband or lover
of his little burden of pleasure; she lifts
the child from his arms, still listening
hard for anything, cradles it
at her breast and begins walking
and rocking. Galway continues to read. And she opens
her blouse to the child and it suckles.

It is an old story. The mother listens,
the fathers listen, the whole audience
listens hard, and when Galway walks away
they lift their hands and their voices, they cup
their hands to hold the very air he breathed
into affirmation, cup their hands to make
the applause a little louder,
a little longer, and truer.

Maryna

I.
Write out if you can
the green of your eyes,
green and clear as marinas
I imagine in southern Spain,
emerald in Greece or Sicily,
clear green through which
we see the shells that stud
the coast with white and pink,
the tones of flesh only sunlight
cares to caress. Travel
when you can the old slow
roads leading from green
into green, the heavy woods
washed in six months' rain.
Cultivate if you can
that ancient Russian pathos,
compassion for melancholy dreams.
And if you can't suppress,
at least resist
the growing taste for vitriol
and pain. So the sea flowers.
Even the mountains are naked
in their wounds. Sadness
and laughter lie together
in beautiful deep lines
like rivers
leading from your eyes.

II.
All week there have been
daffodils, huge yellow
daffodils everywhere I go.
It is Holy Week. The alderbuds
open day by day, the fleshy
shells peal back to reveal
a soft green leaf or two
uncurling from winter sleep.
Each shift of breeze
lets go a cone of seeds
that rattles as it falls.
And when the sun slides out
across the surface of the sea,
high up and slightly south
I see Saturn and Mars alone
in the deep blue bowl of sky,
the one close by, warm red
and pulsing, the other
a distant blue. We
who are nailed to the earth
are lucky—we write out
our lives in water, the
sensual memory of rain,
the gentle suck of the sea.
We taste and smell of earth
and sea. And only rarely
dare speak of the sky.

III.
I thought it was all the years
that held me in their arms,
but it was you, kind sister,
that I could not see
for the sunlight in my eyes.
Like the antique fisherman
of legend, the sunlight spread
its nets across the water and
we saw its shimmering harvest:
salt, fish, the light of day
and dreams of archaic ways.
I thought it was a dream
and it was you in the body
of laughter. All the earth
laughed around us until
I wanted to weep and run
away to hide
like a little horse alone
in a gently sloping pasture
flattened by a storm. Maryna,
the storms of winter perish
in the first blush of spring.
And still we line the days
end to end to topple them
like children topple dominoes
at noon, we scratch the earth
for the roots to a life
that few imagine and no one owns
among the daffodils and crucifixions,
April's cruel traditions.

IV.

So we write out when we can
a whole other life, one
that swells from within. Write out
the voices that you find
curled up inside some dream,
and when your children live
in a strange man's house, one
you thought you had remembered,
write out the mysteries
of a woman alone, a woman
who is a mother. Circe sleeps
in a darkened mist
in the marinas of your eyes.
Odysseus rests beside her.
This journey is by water.
Ride out the voyage even if
it be arduous and long.
You can drift beside a poem
a long long time
before you know it's there,
before its sleepy breath
awakens you from the sleep
of too long being awake.
Let it touch you.
Do not move. You needn't
bother to be brave.
If all its kisses
set you burning, supplicate.
The end is in the journey.

V.
Mnemosyne slumbers
in her chamber, her secrets
all remembered. The Muses
are her daughters. We bend
slowly over the earth
to look at our selves
reflected in the water,
and sudden thirst
overcomes us. The waves
reach out their trembling hands
to touch us and we tremble
in submission. I think
you are like a ship at sea
dragging a tiny fire, riding
the swells like a falling star
ghosting the swells of night.
And no one escapes the night.
Yet we move against the sea
and the sea delivers us
willingly from our selves, away
from harbors and horizons, from
luxurious sorrows toward
a dream or memory, coves
of green light where the surge
of sea is forgotten, where we lose
our selves in the company
of each other, where the sea
and the mountains merge.

In the City of Roses

All night I listened
to the cries of cats
in the alley, their furious
coupling—sounds
like the sobs of children,
yet somehow happy. I lay
on my back on the floor
counting my breaths
as they sliced the dark
like a ripsaw at the end
of a long slow arm
of a god I could not name.

When the first
unwashed fingers of dawn
spread the gray
industrial stacks across
the filthy Willamette,
I remembered again
how the day breaks
with no promise
in a strange town.
I closed my eyes hard
against it, and turned
my face away.

And suddenly, I wanted
to get up and say
something foolish to my friend
asleep a room away,

I wanted to take her two
small hands in mine and
lead her through the streets
where the angels of mercy
hang out their linen
in greasy morning light
among the golden whistles
of factories and the traffic's
messianic hum.
　　　　　　But I rose
and walked to the window—
only the day slowly breaking
over a river that divides
a smoky town
a long way from my home.
If I could offer a heart
or hand, it would grow
like thistle. If I brought
her a gift of roses
to teach her to love
the thorns, my hands
would bloody the lesson.

Nothing will be different
after all. Nothing can change
the gray barges sliding
up the Columbia. Had we
walked down any street,
the small green leaves
would have opened anyway,
the apple burst into blossom,

the swampers arrived
at the bars, the wise
old city curs would have
prowled the rows of garbage.

But I wanted to show her
the roses, how they flourished
among clipped lawns
as I headed out of town,
I wanted to point out
their aching lovely, their
delicate green skins
beneath the armor
of thorns, the thousands
and thousands of actual
non-symbolic, non-archetypal
yellow living roses—
for themselves only, for
what they are.

Many Happy Returns

"There is nothing," you said,
"to return to that
has not been made holy."
Inside the soiled alba
of the human breath
resides an ancient order:
I have returned
to wander the boundaries
of your fingers where
the eclogues sing themselves
a country for the heart.
It's not as easy as that.
If I had wanted only
a measure, I might have paused
to tick the syllables away,
twisted this groan that
passes for a voice into
what song, what agony
of intention. Boundaries
then, where nothing
comes between us.

If I could open my body
like a gate, the pastures
would rise gently toward
dark woods and tall shadows
still or slowly moving. What
goes there goes delicate,
more delicate than speech
or brazen poetry. The heart

is not a gate. What opens
stands ajar already, a mat
of welcome, a temple bell
whose tolling lingers
long, long after the clapper
rests against the air.
When we return into
our bodies, our bodies
change and change,
the candles flicker
in our eyes. This is the forgotten mass,
the one order of old faith,

this is the body, this
is the body and holy, its
eucharist of flesh, its
blessing the holy
of holies for which
we return and return
in the act of worship,
the act of faith.

Gnostology

Each return is a blessing,
a birthing. I come back
again in the last light
of evening and the blue cups
the camas raises to catch
the mist are dripping,
the blackberries turning
blue from green, and down
the narrow Strait of Juan
de Fuca, the foghorns
faintly call. I stand
a long time outside listening
to the dripping of leaves
and nighthawk cries. Behind
me the dark house drips
from the eaves. I slide
the wide door open
and breathe the scents of
stale beer and cigarettes
I smoked last week. The same
books clutter the table.
The same poem dies
in the crude last
unfinished line I couldn't
make to breathe. I ease
into my tattered chair in
trembling light as the sunset
slides into a shadow
ghosting the dark Pacific.
Somewhere, the tide is

staggering over stones at
the feet of incoming swells;
the gulls are scavenging, looping
a last time over the brine
searching for edibles
tangled in the wrack. The moon
slips between two cedars,
razor thin and curved into
a dazzling sliver of ice
simmering in the fog.
The dark of night settles in
on strong steady feet.
The silence is not
profound—it's an old
friend, my beautiful dark
daughter I haven't seen
in years, a longing, a soft
exquisite ache. An hour
flies. Another. My life's
a summer reverie, a dream
that flashes past unnoticed
at the edge of sleep,
a simple gesture: a touch
or kiss of a friend.
                           Finally,
I rise
and step out
of my clothes. I stand
on the porch in the mist,
suddenly naked, lightly
goose-fleshed, more alive
than I have been in days.

My whole body responds
to mist and air, the moist
touch of evening bristling
hairs of belly and legs,
and I feel my nipples'
erection, my scrotum
draw up against my groin,
my toes count every grain
of earth beneath my feet.

Out in the blank space
of night, the thousands
and thousands of systems
are at work lighting
galaxies, whirling the billions
of years into a ball. Are
the ants asleep inside
their catacombs of fir?
Are the chloroplasts
resting their eyes?
With no prayer on my breath,
without hope or fear,
without asking what it is
or what the seasons know,
I gather a long slow breath,
breathe it,
and then I kneel
                    and bow.